BÔ YIN RÂ
(JOSEPH ANTON SCHNEIDERFRANKEN)

VOLUME 12
OF THE 32-VOLUME CYCLE

THE GATED GARDEN

SIGNPOSTS
ALONG THE WAY

For more information
about the books of Bô Yin Râ and
titles available in English translation
visit The Kober Press web site at
www.kober.com

THE KOBER PRESS PUBLISHES THE ONLY ENGLISH TRANSLATIONS
OF THE BOOKS OF BÔ YIN RÂ AUTHORIZED BY THE KOBER VERLAG,
SWITZERLAND. THE KOBER VERLAG PUBLISHES THE BOOKS OF
BÔ YIN RÂ IN THE ORIGINAL GERMAN AND HAS PROTECTED
THEIR INTEGRITY SINCE THE AUTHOR'S LIFETIME.

BÔ YIN RÂ
(JOSEPH ANTON
SCHNEIDERFRANKEN)

SIGNPOSTS
ALONG THE WAY

TRANSLATED FROM THE GERMAN BY
JAN SCHYMURA, MALKA WEITMAN
AND ERIC STRAUSS

THE
KOBER
PRESS

BERKELEY, CALIFORNIA

This book is a translation from the German of *Wegweiser* by Bô Yin Râ (J.A. Schneiderfranken), published in 1928 by Kober'sche Verlagsbuchhandlung, Basel-Leipzig.

The copyright to the German text is held by Kober Verlag AG, Bern, Switzerland.

Printed in the United States of America

International Standard Book Number: 978-0-915034-32-1

Typography and composition by BookMatters

Book cover after a design by Bô Yin Râ

CONTENTS

1 Promise. 1

2 Experience and Phenomenon. 9

3 Knowing and Conveying Knowledge . . 21

4 The Art of Reading. 37

5 On Letters. 49

6 Cults of Personality 61

7 The Urge to Criticize 73

8 Who Was Jakob Boehme?. 87

9 The Gift of Healing. 103

10 The Dangers of Mysticism 115

POEMS

1 The Inner Temple. 131

2 Outer and Inner 132

3 Wisdom. 133

4 Alone and Together 134

5 Water 135

6 It Is Not Easy 136

7 The Eternal 137

8 Sinfonia 138

9 Mysterium Magnum 139

10 Homecoming 140

11 Antagonism 141

12 Foolish Seekers 142

13 False Dignity 143

14 Inner Discipline 145

15 To My Well-Intentioned Friends 146

16 Alignment 147

17 Letting Go 148

18 Blossom or Fruit 149

19 One Thing at a Time 150

20 Know-It-Alls 151

21 Arrogant Ones 152

22 Advice 153

CHAPTER ONE

PROMISE

AUTUMN STORMS HAVE TORN THE LAST few leaves from barren branches.

Withered leaves cover the walkways in a blanket of auburn and gold.

The green leaves that sprouted during springtime and then offered their cool shade from the sultry midday summer sun now lie crushed, moldy, and decaying on the damp ground.

These are the cheerless days when fog rolls in and the sun is often hidden.

Poets say it is "the great dying-off of nature," as they mourn the passing of summer.

But is it true that everything has died?

Are the bare branches really lifeless?

❧

Lift your eyes up off the ground and do not give in to thoughts of death and decay. Then you will behold signs of new life everywhere—and look, over there, the first buds are already sprouting on the hazelnut tree.

No sooner has the last of the fruit been harvested and the last leaf fallen when already there is the promise of a new greening, a new blossoming, the splendor of spring returning in all its beauty.

If even a few warm, sunny days were to arrive you would soon see the first tender buds of green on every bush.

To be sure, ice and storms may still come. How good it is, therefore, that the new buds are shielded from the cold as yet, since the tender life in them must be protected.

As soon as the snow has turned to water and seeped into the furrows of the fields the energy inside the buds—held back in dormant winter—will burst forth with a strength that can no longer be contained.

Each year you await the unhurried, soft approach of spring, and each year you are surprised by the new green life that shoots up overnight.

Just a few sunny days after a warm rain and every branch and twig will be covered in new foliage.

Nature must hold back the life force of its creations for a time in order to protect them from destruction.

Until at last the force of life is freed once more and new growth surges upwards everywhere, arrayed in vibrant color.

∽

Can you not see what nature is teaching you?

You too are not always infused with the source of your inner life and light.

You too have times of ebb and flow determined by your own life's rhythm.

Just when you think you have accomplished everything and feel all too sure of your boundless energy, you are overcome by fatigue. It shakes your confidence—and now all the glowing achievements you were so proud of seem to have lost their luster.

You feel as if the life within you has died, and if you were told that your present lethargy is but a sign that you are gaining new vigor, you would consider that prediction to be nonsense.

You do not understand the rhythms that rule your inner tides and that the unfolding of your spirit ebbs and flows.

Even in the times when you feel farthest from the light, life is stirring in you.

That which is to come is being prepared within you—even if you are unaware of this.

Know this: One day you shall again be as close to the Light as before.

When you have borne the times of dormancy with patience a new resplendent beauty will unfold in you.

Do not give in to feelings of doom and gloom, as if you have nothing left to hope for.

Believe in yourself and be conscious of your inner power, which ceaselessly renews itself.

You create your destiny in those dormant hours and, in the times when you are farthest from the light, seeds are germinating inside you that will unfold in a new spring.

Have confidence in yourself and drive out all impatience from your soul so that in silence the things to come may form themselves.

&

CHAPTER TWO

EXPERIENCE AND PHENOMENON

THE DEGREE TO WHICH WE MAY KNOW truth is determined by our own experiences and their intensity; not by the phenomena that give rise to these experiences.

This observation is self-evident, yet it is little understood.

Most people overestimate the importance of phenomena in determining our experience. At the same time, the capacity for experiencing has atrophied to such an extent that intense sensations and extraordinary external stimuli are often needed to awaken it.

Is it any wonder then that *what* we experience mirrors our diminished capacity to *take in* experience?

That which we experience is merely foam on the surface of the water because we lack the ability to penetrate more deeply into a given phenomenon—even if the thing in question has been dissected by a lancet and its smallest particles analyzed under a microscope.

Even if the physical parameters of an object have been precisely determined by the most exacting scientific method, its "soul" can never be apprehended in this way. The soul of a thing can only be perceived if one's ability to experience has been developed to a level of refinement such that it responds to stimuli that are completely imperceptible to the physical senses.

For such perception to be possible it is irrelevant whether the object is dissected down to its most basic elements—even if only in thought—or whether it is contemplated as a whole.

∞

The depth or significance of an experience is not determined by the magnitude of an object's impact on the physical world or by the scope of a phenomenon.

A display of fireworks may dazzle the eyes and end with a booming grand finale—yet a tiny glow worm in the forest on a midsummer night can inspire in us a far deeper experience than any pyrotechnical artist ever could.

The same applies to all phenomena, regardless of whether perception takes place through sight, sound, or other physical senses.

The majesty of soaring alpine peaks or the wild crashing of ocean breakers can certainly move one's soul but, then again, the smallest, seemingly insignificant things can affect us just as profoundly.

So many individuals—and certainly not just those whose souls have grown cold—are constantly searching for some incredible experience that will shake them to their innermost depths. And because no amount of longing can bring this about, they rush from one phenomenon to another, mistakenly believing that, if only they could have that ultimate, overwhelming experience, it would stir their soul.

As a result, they become familiar with all the world's continents and all of nature's wonders, yet the longing of their soul remains unsatisfied.

Others seek that great fulfillment in the arts, sciences, or abstract thinking, while some, especially nowadays, expect to find their soul's fulfillment in the wonders of technology. Still others seek the thrill of risky sports that overstimulate the senses by playing recklessly with life and death. All such individuals are victims of self-hypnosis; they have convinced themselves that these pursuits can satisfy their yearning.

They do not realize that all such short-lived stimulation, whether refined or crude in nature, will merely numb the soul and betray it. The soul demands the right to feel true joy— the joy that can arise only from a kind of experience in which the soul becomes conscious of itself.

Everyone can find this kind of experience, in abundance, right in their own, immediate surroundings. Once found, all longing for things distant and unknown will appear foolish and the excitement that some believe to be the desired "experience" will only seem a pitiable substitute for *true* experience.

❧

In order to have this true experience, however, one needs to be capable of it.

This capacity is latent in every human being but must be developed through constant practice, or it cannot be accessed.

Utmost concentration is required—a focusing of all one's attention on one point only—and a readiness to enter into such a state of concentration whenever one feels this experience is at hand.

Those who are always seeking distraction will not be able to develop their capacity for such experiences.

They race from one phenomenon to another like insatiable drug addicts. At best, they may realize towards the end of their days that everything they had pursued was folly— and so they breathe their last in bitter resignation.

❧

One should never *search* for true experience nor should one regard it as a gift that can only be received on special occasions.

Genuine experience like this always happens unexpectedly, often in the midst of daily life.

One may set out on a path with a completely different purpose in mind and then suddenly encounter it. But if one starts out with great expectations, one is sure to return home with an empty heart and filled with sadness.

This is true of any experience that brings tidings from the realm of living Spirit.

❧

It is not through manifestations in the physical world that the Spirit may be apprehended but only through experience within. Indeed, the Spirit is an *inner* world of manifestation and thus can only be apprehended within one's innermost. And yet, mortal human beings can only reach this kind of experience *through* phenomena occurring in the physical world.

But when outer phenomena, perceptible to the physical senses, seek to impress you by pretending to be messengers from the world of Spirit, be on your guard. Rarer than diamonds on a seashore are those constellations of energies in which the Spirit manifests itself in sense-perceptible form. And among the millions of humans on earth at any given moment, the number who are able to grasp such phenomena is so tiny that they could all gather in a small room.

Those, however, who have touched the Spirit within their soul's innermost—even if just once—no longer look for it to manifest in phenomena in the physical world. Their inner experience has brought them such great joy that the outer world now appears to them nothing more than illusion compared to the luminous reality that has revealed itself to their soul.

%

It is foolish to believe one has penetrated all the secrets of the material world simply because one has discovered the function of its smallest parts and explored their possible effects—and from these findings created a mental construct, believing that it explains all there is to know about this world. But it is infinitely more foolish to think that the realm of Spirit can be discovered by probing this visible world of manifestation—and it is the height of childish folly if one concludes that, since it cannot be found in this way, it also cannot be found in any other way.

It is no less childish to demand proof of the existence of spiritual forces in the form of some kind of manifestation that can be apprehended by the physical senses.

Those who are still trapped in the labyrinth of their thoughts are very far from understanding the true nature of the realm of Spirit. Indeed, they may even mistake that part of their world of thought that has not yet revealed itself to them but whose existence they can feel—the part that has not yet been incorporated into their labyrinth—for the eternal, radiant Spirit.

Others have heard that the realm of radiant Spirit can only be revealed to them through experience—and now they mistakenly believe themselves to be familiar with this experience because they have experienced it in their *thoughts*.

The experience I am speaking of here has absolutely nothing to do with thought. The realm of radiant Spirit towers above all wonders of the world of thought.

If one wishes to become conversant with some field of human endeavor one needs to fulfill its prerequisites. Similarly, individuals who wish to become open to inner experience need to hone their capacity by using all the possibilities presented by the external world of appearances around them. In this way they may gradually arrive at a point where outer phenomena will bring about those inner experiences that will reveal to them the world of the living Spirit.

Only in one's own soul can this sublime world be experienced—this world which exists beyond the senses and beyond all thought.

Only when one has experienced the world of Living Spirit within one's soul will the world of appearances reveal its inner being—this inner world whose reflection we perceive through our physical senses.

Only through such experience will seekers be able to comprehend the meaning of their own existence, and whatever had until then been shrouded in darkness and hidden from their sight will now shine forth with eternal Light.

❧

CHAPTER THREE

KNOWING AND CONVEYING KNOWLEDGE

I T IS ONE THING FOR ME TO BEHOLD SOME-
thing I see within the clear light of Spirit, and
to understand it for myself alone, and another
to know whether I have also been given the gift
of being able impart what I know to others.

My understanding may be anchored in bot-
tomless depths and yet I may be unable to lift
up the myriad treasures I know to be hidden
there and bring them to the surface.

I may, on the other hand, have long unearthed
such treasures and lifted them up, yet still not
know the art of imbuing them with a luminos-
ity such that skeptical souls would be able to
appreciate their worth and significance.

☙

All this can be easily understood by most people and we see examples of it in everyday life.

Many people who have a strong inner *drive* to teach forget to ask themselves whether they have the *right* to teach.

Many such teachers could make a worthwhile contribution if they taught only what they are capable of teaching. But the troublesome desire to teach things beyond what they are capable of teaching turns them into instruments of harm.

Thankfully, when mundane matters are involved, such a drive to teach can only do limited damage. Those taught by unqualified individuals notice only too soon that they foolishly trusted those they should have spurned.

But in cases where one cannot look to physical reality to correct errors in perception, the influence of those who are driven by the urge to teach can pile up harm upon harm. It may take a long time for these teachers to realize the damage they have done by indulging their passion, and this despite their honest intentions.

Among those striving towards the clear light of Spirit, there are all too many who, the moment they have had their first flicker of spiritual insight, cannot refrain from talking about it and offering unsolicited teaching.

Hardly has the first ray of spiritual light touched them but that they rush through the streets until they find a person willing to be instructed by their paltry knowledge.

They consider themselves to be heralds of the Spirit whereas, in reality, they are merely beguiled by their vanity.

But if any of their new-found pupils dare to voice an objection to the teachings bestowed upon them, because they, in fact, have deeper insights than their benefactor, then these teachers are, unwittingly, exposed in all their poverty. Those who have this urge to instruct cannot conceive of the fact that others they consider to be beneath them could have insights they themselves lack.

The one thing all those addicted to spreading their meager wisdom have in common is their high opinion of themselves.

They use whatever little truth they may have glimpsed to construct a pedestal for themselves from which they may speak from imagined spiritual heights and "look down their noses" at those below.

Little do they realize that they have brought a judgment on themselves. They indeed were called by the Spirit but, now, because of their hubris, they must be excluded from those who are counted among the select by the infallible wisdom of the Eternal.

They do not suspect that their compulsion to teach is their downfall and that they shall never be able to glimpse more than their first glimmers of spiritual insight. They shall never be able to attain the full illumination that brings deepest insight and is granted solely to those who open their mouths to teach only when the Spirit commands them to do so. Even then, those whom the Spirit has chosen to teach are filled with awe and conscious of the almost unbearable responsibility that has been bestowed upon them, and they are hesitant to fit their spiritual insights into the clothing of words.

❧

Alas, if only all those who want to believe that they have a calling to teach could feel even just a little of the sense of responsibility that is felt by those who are truly obligated to teach about spiritual matters.

Even individuals who have only a dim sense of the weight of responsibility borne by those obligated to teach will surely not be so presumptuous as to want to teach others until, beyond every doubt, they feel themselves to be standing in the full light of spiritual knowledge.

&

As I look back on my life, no day fills me with as much awe and trembling as the day I was burdened with the obligation to teach.

It was a shock for me to realize, through my own experience, that it is one thing to be filled with the light of Spirit within one's own soul and quite another to then give form to one's spiritual insights in words, so that they may be absorbed by others.

In those days I often wanted to pray: "Lord, do not lay this burden upon me! Have mercy and select someone else as your servant."*

Such a prayer would have been a sacrilege and would have brought about the annihilation of my spiritual being.

Not one of those who have been called to speak of the Spirit has been spared this terrible hour.

Those who truly may speak of the Spirit because they speak from their own direct experience can scarcely believe that there are others who will casually and audaciously hold forth—when they have not been obligated to do so—about things they have barely discerned.

For those burdened by fate to have to teach from the Spirit, none of the words they write come easily. Even though they have voluntarily offered themselves up for the task, they

---

* This is an allusion to Moses and the Biblical prophets Jeremiah and Jonah who, when God selected them for a mission, protested that they were not worthy and asked God to send someone else.

cannot anticipate the agony that will arise from their earthly limitations.

They feel as if they are standing at a deep well with only a thimble-sized cup in hand, with which they must scoop up water for all who thirst.

Though the water springs from the deepest depths in never-ending abundance, the tiny cup holds so very little of it, and each cup taken from the source is replenished a thousand-fold.

No one is more aware of how powerless they are as mortal humans than those whose duty it is to draw from this well but who are relegated to using a vessel that can hold little more than one can carry in the hollow of one's hand, when they wish to use buckets.

❧

But what is one to make of those who have been moistened by just a droplet of living water and then behave as if they had emptied the entire well?

Human beings may be excused if, upon gaining their first bit of inner knowledge of the Spirit, they are so overwhelmed that they feel

impelled to tell others what they have perceived or think they have perceived.

Not only is such behavior foolish but it is also
wrong as it lacks reverence for the everlasting
Spirit. Even those with just a little common
sense should be able to understand that even
the most astounding inner revelation of spiritual knowledge cannot endow them with the
fullness of all such knowledge all at once—
and that they are not called upon to teach
so long as they, themselves, still need to be
taught.

They may, of course, say to others: "This is
what I was told by those who taught me and
a little of it has been confirmed by my own
experience." However, if they wish to avoid
burdening themselves with heavy guilt, then
they must also have the humility to admit:
"This and that I know, because I have learned
it from another's experience, nevertheless,
it is not knowledge gained from my *own*
experience."

Their own scanty experiences should never
tempt them to give others the impression that they have personally experienced
things that they have merely learned from

teachings—even if they are firmly convinced that what they heard from someone else is just as true as if they had been privileged to experience it within themselves.

Such pretense only impedes inner development and ultimately makes all progress impossible, because everything one ascribes to oneself in the presence of others before having attained it in oneself will cause the very things one strives toward to become unattainable.

Many have adhered to an authentic spiritual teaching and were well on the way to experiencing the Spirit's truth within themselves, but then became agents of their own downfall because they could not refrain from giving others the impression that they had already experienced inwardly what these teachings had yet to lead them to.

❧

The teaching my words convey to the world anew today had already reached souls thousands of years ago, souls who had found confirmation within themselves—through their own experience—of truths they learned through teachings.

These teachings are waiting to be assimilated by ready souls in our time, and more than a few have already found inner confirmation, through their own experience, of what my words seek to convey.

❧

Everything I teach is shared by and belongs to all those who ever were possessed of the fullness of inner wisdom and also those who, in millennia to come, will teach out of their own perfected wisdom. I too had to first come fully into this wisdom before I was allowed to speak of it. But nothing is gained if one merely reads what I have to offer them unless one is also willing to seek confirmation within one's own soul.

Whatever wisdom students of my teachings are able to pass on as a result of their own experience is only of limited value to those who hear them unless these listeners also seek to attain confirmation through experience within *their* own soul.

The ways through which an individual soul may attain such inner confirmation are extremely varied and for this reason I never tire of trying to discover yet another means for inner development and to describe it in my writings.

This is the reason I present the teachings in ever different forms. Each of my small books is made up of different chapters that together form a unity, and each book will appeal and be of help to specific types of souls.

To be sure, everyone can find in each of these small books some things that speak to them. Readers will be drawn to the particular form of teaching that suits the nature of their soul and is therefore meant for them. They will discover what they must demand of themselves and what they can expect from their efforts.

It is not advisable, however, to indiscriminately select from the contents of each of my books and mix them together to create a new framework for one's self. On the other hand, such "mixing and matching" will hardly harm a reader possessed of a mature sense of judgment.

Each book is a unity that I have presented to the world. It is my wish that each book be understood by the reader as a unified whole and that the words of one book not be arbitrarily mixed with another.

The sections of each book should be read and contemplated in the order in which I have arranged them.

This is not to say that one might not come across sentences in one particular book that can be combined with sentences from my other books—indeed, it may be possible to bring together a rich collection of sentences from various of my books that are thematically linked.[*]

I merely wish to warn against the inclination to arbitrarily tear sentences and lines of thought which have a well-founded place within a book out of their context in order to match them with similar ideas from another book and, as a result, end up being given a meaning not intended by me.

I am not concerned about contradictory thoughts being paired—for how can there be any contradictions in my writing when every word flows from the very same well of wisdom? The danger is that something could

---

[*] Such a collection was compiled by a reader of Bô Yin Râ and published in German: Rudolf Schott, *Brevier des Werkes von Bô Yin Râ*, 1965, Kober'sche Verlagsbuchhandlung. The book is currently out of print.

be *perceived* as a contradiction when it was merely presented from a different point of view.

Ultimately, though, the most important requirement for those who have devoted themselves to my teachings is that they act according to the guidance I have given them.

If they do so, my teachings will open for them the path to life in the eternal Light and to the highest knowledge that only comes to those who are perfected in Love.

෯

Just as one should not teach things that one has not yet come to know, one should also not presume to know things that one has grasped only in theory but has not come to understand through inner experience.

How can you know whether what you pass along to others is truth when it has not yet been confirmed for you through your own experience?

Do not take my words as confirmation of the truth of my teachings. Rather, what I teach must prove itself to you through your own incontestable experience of truth.

Only then may you convey to others what I have given to you.

૭૨

CHAPTER FOUR

THE ART OF
READING

NOT EVERYBODY WHO HAS GOOD EYE-sight can also "see." Those who appreciate great works of art have learned to see as artists see.

One must first *learn* to see if one wishes to see as artists do; if one wishes to understand that meadows do not always have to be painted green and oak trees may sometimes be colored blue.

It is not enough to have healthy eyes in order to also "see" in the full sense of the word; one has to learn and practice seeing in the way that artists see.

❧

Is not the same thing true for reading?

All those who learned the letters of the alphabet in school and grew up to take their place among the many average newspaper readers are firmly convinced that they can "read" and, should you have any doubts about their ability, they will read aloud whatever you wish to hear with beautiful pathos in order to prove it to you.

Even so, you will not be able to tell if they can truly *read*.

You will have merely observed that they are able to correctly vocalize combinations of letters and words and sentences.

Real reading is something quite different.

You would be entirely justified in expecting those who claim that they can read to be able to do more than translate letters into words and tell you their correct meaning according to the dictionary, or to analyze sentences grammatically. Above all, they should understand what the author intended to *convey* with these letters, words, and sentences.

This is not an easy thing to do if one relies solely on a sentence one has just read. Most often the reader must consider a particular sentence in the context of the entire written piece, in order to understand its meaning. At other times, perceptive readers will immediately realize that they must disregard all other sentences in order to correctly comprehend a specific, self-contained sentence.

∞

The ability to read presupposes a highly developed intuitive sense.

The reader must have the honest intention to take in what the author has to say and also the ability to enter into the author's thought processes.

If a text deals only with matters that relate to everyday experience or common knowledge, relatively little sensitivity is needed in order to understand it. But things become more difficult when what one is trying to describe is removed from earthly knowledge or experiences with which most people are familiar. In such instances, a correct understanding of the text is impossible without an intense effort to *feel into* its meaning.

We humans are able to make ourselves understandable to each other in that those who know something and wish to convey it to others who do not know it will refer to a reservoir of knowledge and experience that we all share.

Nevertheless, not everyone can or will experience everything and one would have to be ignorant and closed-minded not to acknowledge that fact.

The deeper a person has penetrated into the Spirit, the wider that person's horizon and the more integrous their character, the greater also is their realization that there is still much they cannot reach on their own—though it may nevertheless become accessible to them through the words of others who have already attained it.

The fruit grown in distant lands now gracing your dinner table need not have been plucked by you in order to be savored.

Thus, if you are to understand a text dealing with matters unfamiliar to you, you will be able to ascertain if it is true by absorbing it within yourself—even if, as yet, there is nothing within the scope of your experience to which you can compare it.

The further the writer's experience is from your own, however, the more removed from things that can be perceived in the physical world—the more you will have to try to feel into the author's meaning if you wish to truly understand what has been written.

You must mentally put yourself in the author's place and try to *experience* what the words you are reading are saying, so that you may come near to the experience their author had and is now conveying to you.

Only then may you say of yourself that you know how to read the way every serious person *should* be able to read before they dare attempt to understand words that try to express in language matters of spirit and soul.

This manner of reading will also teach you whether that which you consider to be worth reading truly does have worth. Everything that is empty of value will expose its inner emptiness to you in that it will be unable to sink into the depths your soul. Only writing that has the proper weight will be able to reach this region.

❧

People read a lot these days, perhaps even too much, but only a few truly understand the art of reading.

Newspapers and magazines have destroyed the appreciation of this art. Respect for the book has vanished.

People have grown accustomed to reading in haste, flying over words and sentences, as they do when browsing through the morning papers, so that one scarcely knows any other way of reading anymore.

That a book can be constructed like a temple, that every syllable may form a building block not to be omitted—this realization does not occur to the voracious reader.

Who still remembers the magic of reading, whereby a text is brought to life within the reader and so becomes the reader's permanent, personal possession?

❧

When one reads a book one enters into communion with the author's soul. Readers should therefore select carefully with whom they wish to establish such a relationship.

A book is the magical medium by which mental images conceived by the author are brought into being and then brought to life within the reader. Each mental image you absorb into your soul or even call to mind with pleasure will, in a mysterious way, take part in the shaping of your soul.

Therefore, the choices you make in your reading must be made responsibly.

You should only read texts that inspire mental images within you that foster your soul's highest development.

They need not always be serious books to have this effect.

Humor and satire may awaken within you divine energies which can be invaluable to the shaping of your soul.

Also, there are times when one may benefit greatly from reading books whose value lies solely in the tension which the author manages to produce in the reader.

I certainly do not want to preach a puritanical approach to reading.

If you wish to read, then read whatever you chose to read—but do so as one who consciously experiences the miracle whereby lines of strange symbols on a piece of paper stimulate your own creative powers so that the same mental images that once were formed in another human being's soul now arise in yours.

Learn to have reverence for the word.

A single page read with care, so that every word is clearly understood in its full meaning, will bring you more gain than if you had read the best of books quickly and in one sitting, hardly paying attention to individual sentences, let alone individual words.

Only when you have learned to read as one ought to read will a book truly belong to you.

The manner in which you read a book, the depth of your understanding, will transform its words so that your perceptions of its meaning will be different from any other reader.

A book may come to hold value for you at a level that exceeds the meaning that is obvious to most people.

Indeed, by reading a book as one *ought* to read, your soul may be enriched even more than that of the author who created it.

I advise you to venture to read a book in this way. If you can do so with full consciousness and not let yourself slip back into old habits then you will surely never wish to read in any other way.

The effort that is required of you is modest and the gain that may be yours is great.

Even light reading and humor require that you pay close attention to every word, for how else can they reveal their essence to you and thus partake in the formation of your soul? How can you become conscious of the energy embedded in the words if you simply fly over the sentences in great leaps and bounds? If you do not take the time and care to find every possible meaning in the text, you will never discover the value that the writing may hold for you.

"Learning to read" means that you respect yourself as a reader and consider yourself too good for fruitless pursuits.

Once you have mastered the art of reading, everything you read will bring you rich reward.

CHAPTER FIVE

ON LETTERS

THERE IS SOMETHING MYSTERIOUS ABOUT a piece of paper covered in strange symbols which, when sent from one person to another, conveys the sender's thoughts and feelings to the recipient.

But because the exchange of letters has become so common in everyday life, we have lost the ability to sense the mystery. It takes a conscious effort to get beyond our conventional thinking and to be able to sense that mystery once again.

The mystery inherent in letters goes beyond the wondrous process by which a thought may be set down in those symbols we call an alphabet, such that this thought can be released time and again by the act of reading—a process that takes place with any written communication.

We are dealing, rather, with an invisible, fluidic element which can only be perceived through *feeling*. It reaches the recipient and is taken in, together with the piece of paper and its symbols, whether the person is conscious of this or not.

∾

Every person possessed of some sensitivity can feel this fluidic element as clearly as they are able to see the symbols with their eyes. Those who do not feel it are affected by it nonetheless—they are merely unaware of its effects.

It matters little whether a letter has been written by hand or with the help of a mechanical apparatus as long as it comes from the writer's own hand, that is, not first prepared for the printing press and then printed onto different paper.

The paper itself carries the fluidic element and this element would be transmitted even if the sender were only to "think his or her thoughts" onto the paper instead of writing them down.

The content of a letter consists not only of what the written words say but, even more so, the fluidic element which can be *felt* and which may actually convey the opposite of what is written.

Thus, a letter may only be properly appreciated when it comes directly from the writer, and only at the moment it is opened. This is because the fluidic element dissipates so quickly that, after just a few days, hardly any of it can still be felt.

A letter is intended only for the person to whom it was written. Recipients will always absorb the accompanying fluidic element unless they feel the need to protect themselves and therefore consciously defend against it.

※

Knowing all this, how can one justify the pervasive, shameless practice of digging up the correspondence of all kinds of people, important or not, using some specious pretext, in order to exploit it and publish yet another book because today's flood of publications is just not enough for some people.

So as not to leave any room for doubt, let me clearly state that I find little in this world as reprehensible as the desecration of the dead that is perpetrated by posthumously publishing their letters.

Those writers who lust after fame but have absolutely nothing of importance to say seek renown by publishing the letters exchanged by some literary figure. As a result, Mr. or Ms. Nouveau Riche can amass an entire library of such publications and, after thumbing through a few of these tomes, may appear to be well informed without ever having read a single line of an actual book written by the author in question.

Unfortunately, the deceased letter writers cannot defend themselves from being plundered—and it is plunder whether publishers are dragging forth these old letters to gain personal renown or believe they are honoring the author.

∞

The popular craze for publishing the correspondence of individuals who are considered to be important may lead to a kind of cultural misunderstanding. When letters are unearthed from where they reposed and made accessible to strangers for whom they were not intended, the reader may come to incorrect conclusions as to their meaning. This is because one can never know the context in and circumstances under which the letters were originally written.

Moreover, an exchange of letters that was originally the concern only of the immediate correspondents is a questionable source of insight for later, uninvited readers. Later readers cannot evaluate the meaning of these letters with objectivity; their own subjective feelings color their understanding, much as they might want to deny this. They may not even be aware of their inherent bias.

The exceptions to this rule are letters of very general content such as descriptions of travels or current events, humorous essays, love letters, or letters that convey factual information or instructions. In such cases it matters little whether the reader approaches the words with objectivity or identifies with the feelings of the writer.

☙

There are also, of course, letters that actually appear to have been written for the purpose of later publication.

In such cases we are no longer dealing with that mysterious bridge that connects one person with another. Rather, these are simply essays in letter form. If someone who has something to say wishes to use this format for some reason there is, of course, nothing wrong with this.

Lamentably, and in violation of the private nature of a true letter, one may still find individuals who do not consider it beneath their otherwise carefully tended dignity to craft their supposedly intimate, private letters with a view to possible later publication.

Here we see yet another expression of human vanity, not to mention a demonstration of rather questionable taste.

∞

If letters are to become again what they were in better days for many spiritually mature individuals, such individuals will have to find their way back to an open and candid way of writing to each other. A letter's content is nothing more than arid information if its words do not flow from a truly opened heart—and a letter will never open the recipient's heart if that person can sense that the words were chosen, not for him or her, but with a view to future publication.

If a letter is to accomplish what a true letter can, it must issue forth from that region of a person's innermost in which we all find our common, eternal home, and must be written for the addressee alone.

This singular focus on a particular "you" is the essential characteristic of a true letter.

A letter written to many loses its principal strength and is not, strictly speaking, a real letter anymore but, rather, a circular, report or a treatise.

It goes without saying that I am not referring here to business correspondence, although these letters too need not be as impersonal as some businesspeople seem to believe. The great "princes" of commerce have long realized that one can accomplish more with letters that are personal in tone—something the old Hanseatic merchants knew and practiced.

✺

What I have in mind here is to see the letter restored to its venerable role as an important means of encouraging and uplifting each other on the spiritual path.

This goal can only be achieved by freeing oneself from clichéd writing and from any reticence in one's expression that is driven by self-consciousness or anxiety.

This does not mean, however, that one should immediately lay one's most intimate revelations at the feet of every untried person. Indeed, it requires a certain amount of tact to be able to find just the right words and the suitable tone for each individual.

And yet, our earthly lives would be immeasurably enriched if it were possible to, once again, trust that each letter one receives is a sincere expression of its writer's inner world.

It is true that the conditions of modern life prevent us from returning to the blessed time when there was leisure to spend time with each letter—when one would wait weeks for the post to arrive and again more weeks before being able to post the answer.

Nevertheless, even nowadays one should not feel compelled to hurry an exchange of letters.

The fact that one *can* reply at once does not mean that one *must* do so.

Though it may be more difficult than in former times to find the leisure for correspondence, even today, a letter need not show the signs of haste which our modern age accepts as the normal pace of life.

❧

CHAPTER SIX

CULTS OF
PERSONALITY

As long as human beings live upon this earth no one will be able to change the fact that certain individuals who contribute to the well-being of all, or at least appear to do so, are thanked and even revered by those of their fellows who feel personally touched by their actions.

There is gratitude for help received; there is reverence when those who have benefited from that help feel themselves uplifted to heights which they could not have attained on their own yet felt, intuitively, were within human reach.

Who would object to an expression of such gratitude or reverence, when genuine help has been received?

These two emotional responses are deeply rooted in every human being—unless that person is completely debased—and it is easy to see how significant such feelings are for the preservation of the species and for the unfolding of that which is most noble within a people.

∾

Gratitude and reverence go awry, however, when they are no longer guided by reason— when one abandons one's ability to make selective judgments and indiscriminately reveres anyone who has qualities that exceed one's own.

As a result, the strong man of the fairground booth, the juggler and the fire-eater may be held in the same reverence as one who creates works that express the highest spiritual values. Likewise, all distinction between true art and stunts that are artfully performed may be lost.

But even when one reveres another who embodies the highest values, one must guard against allowing that reverence to deteriorate into a cult of personality. One must remain ever cognizant of how easily reverence of a person may cross the line into idolization, and fight against the dangerous impulse to revere a personality more than the contributions that person has made.

∾

The vast majority of people attain importance only for themselves and their immediate circle and only a few become important for the larger society—perhaps even for all of humanity—because they serve as role models for the noblest within all of us.

One can understand that those who have importance for humanity are shown more reverence than those who are important for only their immediate circle, even if that circle is quite significant in a particular area of human endeavor.

The danger lies in confusing that which is worthy of reverence with the mortal human being who gave it shape and form in the material world.

One may respect, even esteem, a person who has produced something worthy of reverence and consider it a miracle that a fellow human being has fully lived up to the highest level of inner development. Nevertheless, one must always carefully distinguish between that which a person has attained and the mortal human they remain despite everything: between the impersonal values of the spiritual realm and the personal attributes of the individual who exemplifies such values and who has been able to embody them through arduous labor or the gift of grace.

One should also never forget that those who bring spiritual values into being in the material world are only creators in as much as they draw from the abundance the world of Spirit has revealed to them, just like one draws water from a mighty river. They do not create something out of nothing.

In the same way, everything that individuals draw from the abundant well of the Spirit and make accessible to their fellow human beings is a Revelation, be it the result of long years of experimentation or the gift of a divinely-inspired moment.

To idolize those individuals is foolish and, beyond that, denigrates their deed or work. It also disrespects the very person one is idolizing because it imposes on the idolized person a false belief that they themselves might strenuously reject.

∾

Whenever an individual contributes something meaningful to their fellow human beings one must ask whether the value of that contribution stands or falls with that individual's existence on this earth or whether, instead, some aspect of it—some creative work or deed that continues to bear fruit or to give direction to humanity—remains alive after the bearer of these gifts is no longer present and working in this material realm.

There is never a reason to idolize those who make outstanding contributions to humanity or to pay homage to their person, even if one considers this concept in the lofty sense Goethe conceived it.* Those whose accomplishments have truly been valuable for humanity will always reject such idolization and look upon it with embarrassment and even

---

* Goethe was a voice for the ideals of liberal humanism, which emphasized the individual's freedom of choice, responsibility to shape one's life according to the highest moral standards and to continuously evolve as a person of character.

disgust, even though they by no means underestimate their importance to the world.

Those who are truly influential in this world understand, deep within themselves, the nature and degree of their importance.

They would be false to themselves and to others were they to play at being modest and pretend not to recognize their own significance.

Such individuals are aware of their importance and yet understand that they are only intermediaries for the work. They endure the reverence, even awe of others in the same spirit as a diplomatic envoy accepts the honor paid to his or her country. They do not, however, use their contribution to put their own person in the spotlight and thus shift the focus away from the value of the work.

ॐ

When individuals make contributions that elevate the spiritual lives of their fellow human beings, one can understand why they often feel compelled to prove, as best as possible, that they are not offering stolen goods but have come by the treasures they possess in legitimate ways.

Whether what they offer actually derives from the realm of radiant Spirit can only be determined by "trying on" the gift itself to see whether it is what it claims to be. One should never simply trust the giver's word that it was acquired in a legitimate way. The way in which it was acquired is always very important.

Contributions of true value that have their source in the realm of pure, living Spirit can never be attained through mental speculation or scientific investigation. On the other hand, it would be both irrational and presumptuous to expect something that can only be achieved through intense mental effort to come to us effortlessly from the realm of Spirit.

But just as the discovery of a chemist has value in itself, regardless of who the scientist's teachers were or what factory produced the equipment used, so too must that which has been bestowed by the Spirit also have value in itself regardless of how the person who has brought it into the world tells us it was acquired or even who they claim to be.

૭૦

One must never accept what is bestowed by the Spirit solely on someone else's authority—I cannot caution strongly enough against this. Whoever accepts things on the word of another that should only be confirmed *through one's own, inner experience* is naive and runs the risk of being defrauded and left with counterfeit goods, or purchasing pinchbeck instead of gold.

Cults of personality create the ideal hothouse conditions in which the inclination to accept things on authority, instead of upon inner examination, can flourish.

❧

Far from such idolization is the trust human beings place in a true mediator of the Spirit's light.

Just as one ought to purchase expensive items only from merchants whose credibility and sound judgment in selecting their merchandise have been well-proven, so too, one should never accept spiritual goods from persons one cannot firmly trust. And beyond this, one must still not relinquish the right to first test the value of what has been received within one's own, innermost being.

Once one has repeatedly verified that the gifts of another are authentic and worthy of trust, one can feel confident that what they offer in the future will also be authentic and worthy of trust. In time, one's own ability to judge may become honed and even equal the level possessed by the mediator one has come to trust—just as art collectors may gradually acquire an eye for what is genuine without the use of experts or specialized testing methods.

This analogy further illustrates the point I am making here: When evaluating spiritual teachings, the essential thing is what the teacher conveys. Focus on the teaching and do not idolize the person.

There are art collectors who have a preference for a particular master who represents a particular style or period and make every effort to acquire this artist's work.

Such collectors may honor the artist who created the works, but only because of the vision that enabled this unique human being to create them.

No one would consider this honoring to be a cult of personality.

Collectors of spiritual treasures must also proceed in this way.

Although they may venerate those who bring them gifts from the Spirit, that veneration should be inspired by the value of the gifts themselves—and here, perhaps also because genuine emissaries from the realm of living Spirit are seldom found and are far more rare than genuine artists.

☙

CHAPTER SEVEN

THE URGE TO CRITICIZE

WITH REGARD TO CERTAIN DISEASES whose symptoms are known to neurologists, the curious observation has been made that such affected persons inwardly oppose any cure; they consider their condition to be a sign of worth and, therefore, do not wish to be liberated from it.

Far too many people nowadays have been infected by a similar pestilence—they have been taken over by a compulsion to criticize. They no longer feel comfortable unless they can constantly find cause to negate the actions of their fellow human beings for reasons that may be justified or, as is more often the case, completely unjustified.

Those suffering from a compulsion to criticize forget that normal, healthy criticism is justified only when one is sure of one's knowledge of the matter in question or when one is informed enough to evaluate whether someone's actions may hinder their intended objectives or have unethical motives.

శ్రీ

Criticism that is motivated by a healthy urge to criticize is always benevolent and seeks either the well-being of the person criticized or the good of those needing to be protected from such a person.

Those whose criticism is healthy and constructive will never stubbornly adhere to their own opinion and will always be amenable to being corrected by someone with superior knowledge.

Those whose urge to criticize is unhealthy and compulsive seek only their own gratification and feel frustrated when their hunger, one could almost say lust, is not satisfied in the usual way.

Many are not clear about this distinction and over-indulge their once healthy critical impulses to the extent that being critical becomes a habit. They come to take pleasure, and even pride themselves, in finding fault with everything their fellow human beings do because their original, healthy critical instincts have become corrupted.

What I say here also concerns those whose urge to criticize is still healthy, because awareness of how healthy criticism can become corrupted is the best protection against this danger.

⚭

There is a certain undeniable, sensual pleasure in loosening the reins of one's desire to criticize and enjoying the response that unrestrained negation will always elicit in others, either in the form of agreement or indignant defense.

It is precisely this temptation that must be resisted because those who succumb to it will not be able to maintain the health of their critical instincts.

This is not some harmless game which need not be taken seriously.

Far too much harm is wrought through rash and arrogant criticism that is the result of a pathological urge to criticize that has become destructive. It is high time to resolutely confront this evil.

I am not talking about professional critics who deal with art, literature, music, or theater. For the most part, these critics are journalists who are sufficiently knowledgeable about their fields to be able to criticize in a way that is constructive and may even fertilize the creativity in these art forms.

⚭

One is unlikely to come across anyone suffering from a compulsion to criticize among professional critics, and so their judgments, even when negative or erroneous, do not have the power to destroy. The criticized work still continues to exist and, in the course of time, may be reevaluated and seen in a different light.

Things are quite different with regard to the quarrelsome pronouncements on the words and deeds of others by those whose urge to criticize knows no restraint. Here ignorance, disrespect, or ill will can stifle expression right from the start so that there is never even an opportunity for re-evaluation in the future.

This applies especially to the public sphere, where countless individuals regard their right to have a say in the social and political arrangements that affect their lives as a license to criticize indiscriminately.

Especially here, in the public sphere, such degeneration is contagious and can escalate into an epidemic.

When everyone feels they are entitled to criticize the words and deeds of others, even if they lack expertise of the subject at hand, a ripple effect is created. Through the power of suggestion, one person's fault-finding invites the next person's and the next, each person's pronouncements building on the preceding ones. Needless to say, in such instances vanity rules, and the inflation of such critics' own personalities becomes more important than objectivity.

∂

Those who have succumbed to this epidemic love to use slogans because they are an easy, yet powerful, way to make a point.

Even the most ignorant can become expert in the use of slogans—always sure bait with which to catch those who are too lazy to think and too immature to form their own opinion.

When critics rely on slogans as a means of winning people over, the weakness of their argument is unmasked and one can be certain that they are simply using slogans to make their own deficient intellect appear impressive and important.

Indeed, it would be accurate to say that criticism loses its credibility to the same degree as the critic resorts to the use of catchy slogans.

Those whose criticism is healthy rarely use slogans.

Such healthy critics are guided first and foremost by a sense of responsibility.

A healthy critical urge is not about emphasizing the personality of the critic but, rather, about perfecting a situation, service, or some other kind of human endeavor.

∞

The critical impulse is unique to human beings, and elevates them above animals.

Even the most intelligent animal accepts its environment as it is and does not have the impulse or capacity to find fault with it or to conceive of something better.

An animal will respond to its environment with happiness and acceptance or with aversion and resistance, but these responses are merely manifestations of its survival instinct and not value judgments.

The human being's critical urge presupposes a memory of a more perfect state of existence; more perfect than could ever be encountered here on earth.

If this material world were the only and true home of human beings, as it is for animals, how would it be possible for humans to feel unsatisfied and thus find fault with their existence?

It is solely because the Spirit that dwells within human beings knows and remembers a more perfect realm that humans can feel unsatisfied and critical of their circumstances on this earth.

Although we are no longer conscious of the existence we experienced when we were united with the light of Spirit, which is our true and original home, the memory of this more perfect existence is, nonetheless, the reason we feel dissatisfied and find fault with our surroundings here on earth.

Our original Being—the timeless entity composed of spiritual substance that we are—turned away from oneness with the light of pure Spirit and towards outer experience, moving through ever denser worlds until finally becoming embodied on this earth. Cast out of the radiant realm of pure Spirit, the timeless spiritual substance—now housed within the mortal, human being—experiences itself only through the *physical* senses. Nevertheless, it retains a memory of its former, pure state of being. Even though the physical brain cannot call this memory up into consciousness without intentional preparation, it is always vaguely aware of and influenced by it.

All expressions of a healthy critical urge result from comparing, on an unconscious level, a given, imperfect physical state with the absolute perfection of the corresponding state in the realm of Spirit.

Here on earth we human beings are pulled by two very different visions of what the ideal existence should look like. We may chose to ignore this duality but, unless our feelings have become completely petrified, we suffer bitterly from this tension nonetheless.

If we were only physical beings then there would be no such duality in what we strive towards in this life and none of the suffering that comes with it.

Thus, while our bodies tell us with brutish insistence what they need and want to feel completely satisfied, our brains simultaneously receive purely spiritual influences that point us towards a vision of perfection in the light of which all things on earth must, necessarily, appear to us as flawed.

If we seek to perfect things that are subject to physical laws according to an ideal that can only be realized in the realm of the Spirit, we will be filled with inner discord.

This includes all attempts to "spiritualize" the body.

Instead, we have been offered the sublime possibility of *embodying the Spirit* while still abiding in the earthly realm. However, we can only do so within the limits imposed by our physical senses and our experience will of necessity seem imperfect compared to the perfection that exists in the spiritual realm.

❦

Because the urge to criticize is begotten of the Spirit but impacts only this physical realm, we mistakenly assume that we can shape material things to a degree of perfection that is only possible in the realm of Spirit.

Hence the unrealistic demands we place on ourselves and others; hence the contagious nature of an unrestrained critical urge.

Those who can understand what is to be understood here should realize once and for all that criticism of the pursuits of their fellow human beings can only be justified, and the critical urge can only remain healthy, if one takes care to evaluate these pursuits in the light of the conditions imposed on human endeavors here on earth.

Even the most perfect human achievement within the physical world of manifestation remains imperfect compared to the perfection that exists within the realm of Spirit.

How much greater the need for forbearance, therefore, in circumstances where even earthly perfection cannot realistically be expected.

❧

The compulsion to criticize is the affliction with which the serpent of paradise infected humanity.

And now, having read this far, perhaps you can better understand the implications of the seductive words the serpent—the satanic principle in the mythic tale—says to human beings: "...ye shall be as gods, knowing good and evil." (Genesis 3:5 KJV)

The "gods" who are privy to such "knowledge" are cheerless and ultimately mortal.

In the presence of the timeless, living Spirit, however, all evil is a temporal and transient aberration. Within the realm of Spirit, perfection alone exists and comes to consciousness—the primordially begotten Good that eternally begets itself anew—and evil is "non-being," without reality.

❧

Lastly, a word about self-criticism.

Those who are overly self-critical will be the first to understand that, just as with criticism of another, over-indulgence in criticism of oneself can become destructive if not guided by right wisdom and restraint.

Criticism of one's own attitude and behavior can help or hinder oneself, just as our criticism of others may help or hinder them.

In both cases, criticism will only be a source of blessing if that which is good is recognized and valued before looking for the faults and shortcomings in oneself or others.

A single positive quality can outweigh a multitude of shortcomings.

The biblical tale tells us that Sodom was destroyed because of the sins committed by thousands of its inhabitants—but had it been possible to find even just ten righteous people, God would have spared the entire city for their sake (Genesis 18:16-33).

❧

CHAPTER EIGHT

WHO WAS JAKOB BOEHME?

WHO WAS JAKOB BOEHME? IT MAY SEEM superfluous to ask this question, as it has been asked many times by others and at other times.

Past and present interpreters of the curious work bearing the name "Boehme" have sought, with more or less success, to decipher the nature of the person behind these writings.

People who have never read a single line that Boehme wrote seem to know that he—apart from who he truly was—could also make shoes. Some interpreters of his work refer to him as "the shoemaker of Goerlitz"—a description that is, at best, a matter of personal preference. Others who take my point of view feel differently and agree that, although shoemaking is indeed an honorable craft and those who practice it can be most proud of their famous fellow guild member, emphasizing Boehme's work-a-day occupation does not give one any sense of the great spiritual depth of the author of these profound disclosures about spiritual matters.

Of course, there have always been those to whom the essence of this person who has been so significant for the spiritual development of humanity is not defined by the way he earned his living in this world and who thought it irrelevant that he had grown up without the education typical in his day.

Boehme's writings, however, reveal only too clearly how much he regarded his lack of education as an obstacle. All his life he struggled to grasp the terminology used by his scholarly friends in order to convey his thoughts and spiritual insights in language they would better understand.

Everything we know about Boehme's life shows us that he considered the need to ply his trade a constant distraction and how much he tried to gain his freedom in order to devote himself completely to the inner promptings of his lofty spirit.

If one truly wishes to fathom the spiritual treasures within the earthly shrine that was the person of Jakob Boehme, one must not approach the writings of this sage with the preconceived notion that they consist of the homespun speculations of an honest crafts-man at his workbench who has forgotten that he is there to make shoes, but instead has preferred to seek answers to metaphysical questions that have disturbed the peace of his pious soul.

My words are intended for all those who know the name of this sage but have not read his writings or, perhaps, laid them aside too quickly because they were uncomfortable with his unusual and singular way of express-ing himself.

Those who have studied Boehme's writings in earnest and have made the effort to familiarize themselves with his language and to under-stand the intended meaning of his words will also have learned to bow in reverence before the man who was allowed to write such texts. Those who have experienced this reverence confirm that it arises in them as they begin to unveil the treasures contained in Jakob Boehme's cosmic writings, and feel their own soul echo the wondrous depths that Boehme is revealing to them.

To be sure, we are only speaking here of Boehme's knowledge of the radiant world of Spirit.

It is true that he often erred when he wrote about the physical universe, relying on knowledge borrowed from others, and that his conclusions were limited by what was known in his time. And yet, despite all this and the rigid, religious dogmas that fettered him, here we behold one of the wisest among all who ever sought to fathom the primal depths of ultimate human knowledge.

He was a "well-digger" who deepened the shaft of his well so that it reached down to the very primordial waters of life.

❧

Whoever summons the courage to climb down the shaft of this well—for there is no bucket fastened on a rope with which one might draw up some water—will realize that one only needs to build a shaft of equal depth inside *oneself* in order to come upon the same living waters within one's own soul.

However, those who are caught in the religious myths that cling like tangled roots to the walls of the shaft that Boehme built in himself—ready to enmesh unsuspecting seekers—should feel fortunate if they are able to free themselves again. Although the waters of the deep will still only reflect back to them their own unsettled countenance.

∾

All this I needed to say before I could answer the question as to who this remarkable seer was—so wise, in his own way, about the realm of Spirit. Recent research has finally accorded him the respect he deserves in the intellectual history of humanity. However, he never lacked admirers who were amazed by one or the other facet of his person and writings—though none were able to comprehend the entirety of this great human being's nature.

The answer that it is my obligation to now provide applies only to the origins of Boehme's spiritual development and insights, which have been revealed to me and which I know to be to be irrefutably true. My assertions will be understandable to those who have recognized that all workings of the Spirit here on earth are the final effects of sublime impulses, born of compassion, that have their origin in the realm of radiant Spirit.

I ask the reader to bear in mind what I have already mentioned countless times, namely, that the divine may only be grasped by humans through the human spirit and that all influence that humanity receives from the realm of radiant Spirit issues from an invisible Temple here on earth. Its foundation stones consist of human beings who dwell simultaneously in the realm of pure Spirit and on earth, fully and continuously conscious in both realms.

It was from this invisible Temple that Boehme received his guidance and was led to work on behalf of the Spirit.

As a pupil of the spiritual circle working in seclusion while living simultaneously here on earth and in the realm of Spirit—which I have often described elsewhere—he ascended from level to level as far as was possible for him during his life on earth, knowing full well from whence his illumination came.

☞

He was commanded to keep silent about the source of his insights and not reveal them to the outside world.

He himself was not destined to take his place as a Luminary within the circle of the Luminaries of Eternal Light.

The flames of earthly needs and desires still burned within him, dimming the white-golden light of the divine Spirit that was his core being, for he had not undergone the millennia of spiritual development that every Luminary must have completed before he can be incarnated in a mortal body.

And yet, Jakob Boehme's work shows the world what a truly worthy person who has been accepted to become a pupil of the Light can achieve—even though the world could not know the source from which his power flowed.

It was impossible for the interpreters of Boehme's writings to know the truth as to the origin of his ability as a seer. Nor was it possible for them to so much as suspect that he was receiving spiritual guidance of a kind known to very few on earth, and those few were bound to silence.

And yet it is not impossible to imagine that Boehme may have alluded to the source of his insights with trusted friends, in a way that seemed to him permissible. This would explain the account we have from his first biographer,* which I will describe below— although nowadays people don't know what to make of it and tend to believe it is little more than an attempt to build a myth around Boehme.

Boehme's biographer and friend knew enough about his subject's insights to write the following:

"It may well be that from an *external* source, through the *magical-astral* workings of *heavenly* spirits, some *hidden* sparks and glimmers like unto Love's holy fire were *embedded....*"**

---

* Abraham von Franckenberg, *The Life and Death of Jacob Behmen*, 1651. Translated by Francis Okely, 1780.

** In the German original, Bô Yin Râ added a footnote here explaining that he has added the emphasis to certain "words that matter" that was not present in the original text. The implication in this quote is that the "sparks and glimmers" were embedded in Boehme's writings.

One would not be amiss to assume that the biographer suspected some things about the circumstances behind Boehme's writings or perhaps that he even knew more, as a result of what Boehme had intimated, than he was willing to say.

Those who have understood the real source of Boehme's insights will no doubt find it striking that, following the above excerpt, the biographer recounts how on one occasion "a stranger, shabbily dressed but, nevertheless, a refined and honorable man, entered the shop in which Boehme was working as a young apprentice." He then tells us that Boehme was alone at the time and that suddenly this man, who Boehme did not know at all, addressed him by his name, greatly startling him.

The text then continues:

"Then the man, whose mien was serious and kind and whose eyes seemed to sparkle with light, clasped his right hand and looking him full in the face said: 'Jakob, thou art little, but thou shalt become great, and a man very different from the common cast...'"

"Upon which the man pressed his hand again and looked him full in the face, left and went on his way."

The author goes on to tell us that after this meeting Boehme did indeed become different and that "shortly thereafter followed his inner illumination, the knowledge of his spiritual calling and his Sabbath Day."

∞

Though I am far from wanting to pass judgment as to what weight one should give this story, I believe that I should not omit certain salient information that will orient the reader.

Since I have not set myself the task of interpreting Boehme's writings I shall not recount other stories here, although it is possible that those who are thoroughly familiar with these writings could point out other mystery-filled passages that would be worth mentioning.

Let it suffice that I have drawn the reader's attention to the above.

What I shall offer here—and what can only be obtained from a unique source—is an explanation regarding the origin of Boehme's spiritual maturity. I was prompted to write this because I have observed, over and over again, that even the best interpreters of this remarkable manifestation of the Spirit, Jakob Boehme, have been unable to fully understand either the human being or the writings as long as they remain unaware of the relationship of Boehme to the spiritual circle I have referred to as the Luminaries of Eternal Light.

෨

The reasons that once bound the wise seer to silence have long since lost their relevance and Boehme's writings become far more accessible if one also understands the origin of his spiritual insights and is therefore able to discover its traces throughout his work.

The temporal and all too personal influences in his work may be laid aside without diminishing the essence of his writings. These influences stem from the fact that he had to accommodate the belief systems of the world in which he lived—or risk enduring far harsher suffering than he was already subjected to at the hands of those who adhered to the beliefs dominant in his world.

Although written more than three hundred years ago,[*] the core of his writings—when stripped of these outside influences and laid bare—is also just as meaningful for the present day.

It can never become outdated because it issues from the realm of Eternity—the ever-present, timeless *now*.

Jakob Boehme used words to give form to the visions of his soul, so that he might better grasp and remember them. He was, after all, not lord and master of what his soul beheld but, rather, had always to wait until the realm of Spirit would open up to him again. Thus, there was always the danger of losing what had been granted to him.

No wonder then that the essential elements of his writings were often embellished in a bizarre and confusing manner. This arabesque style was the only way he could express the inexpressible.

Colorful expression was common in his day and also suited his nature. Thus, he forced his language to express his vivid experiences and

---

[*] This book was originally published in German in 1928.

it mattered little to him if the words resisted his efforts to encompass the overflowing abundance of his inner visions.

Only by lovingly immersing oneself in Boehme's work will one be able to extract the treasures its words contain.

❧

CHAPTER NINE

THE GIFT OF
HEALING

But when the multitudes saw it, they
marvelled, and glorified God, which had
given such power unto men.
                    —Matthew 9:8 KJV

IT HAS BEEN REPORTED THAT A MAORI tribesman in New Zealand is able to bring about astounding healings and cures for the sick. He is said to be a baptized Christian who asks those seeking to be healed by him to give thanks not to him, but to the Holy Trinity: the Father, the Son, and the Holy Spirit. In fact, he warns that the cure may not last if they fail to maintain this faith.

In Christian circles the healings performed by this Maori tribesman were viewed as concrete evidence of the truth of the dogma of the Holy Trinity.

Then in Europe there was Émile Coué, who asked nothing more of sick individuals than to believe in the power of their own imagination. His results, using this approach, were equally marvelous.

And following close upon this, now there is news of a healer who is said to bring about cures for all kinds of sicknesses simply by the laying on of his hands.

This time the healer is a Buddhist monk, reportedly Chinese but working in India. And although India is a country quite accustomed to "miracles," he has aroused astonishment and awe with his cures.

As the number of sick who came to him grew, it became increasingly impossible for him to lay hands on each one of them, so he decided to transmit his healing power to five of his pupils.

Newspaper reports indicate that the genuineness of the cures is indisputable and therefore—as is usual in such cases—people are mystified.

To be sure, one hears news of miraculous cures from East Asia from time-to-time although, upon closer examination, very few of these can be verified despite the fact that there is never a lack of "credible eye witnesses."

But the reports of the healings by the Buddhist monk are not beyond the scope of what a reasonable person can believe.

※

I am astonished that time and again people are amazed and at a loss for explanations when they hear of such cures. In some circles one even hesitates to give credence to the sympathetic and sober Mr. Coué, who certainly never sought to ascribe anything miraculous to his person or his cures.

Mr. Coué spoke only of "autosuggestion," whereas here I am writing about the actual healing energies that autosuggestion unshackles. Still, the essence of his attempt at explanation is that all human beings carry within themselves energies that can heal.

No doctor on earth can really cure someone except by activating these internal energies. This is the case whether the doctor uses medications or surgical intervention to heal the patient.

These ideas are nothing new. Since time out of mind people have realized that a doctor can only stimulate nature's healing powers but is otherwise unlikely to accomplish much, even using the best medicines or by removing the diseased organ.

There are, however, other factors at play here and Mr. Coué's modest assertion that he has nothing to do with the cures he achieves and that he merely teaches patients how to help themselves should not be taken as absolute truth—even if Mr. Coué deeply believes this to be true.

The personality of the healer is always of decisive importance, regardless of what method is used for healing. It matters not whether one uses autosuggestion as popularized by Mr. Coué and practiced for almost half a century by the American New Thought Movement,* faith healing, the laying on of hands, or medical or surgical interventions.

---

*The New Thought Movement developed in the United States in the 19th Century. It holds that God or infinite intelligence is everywhere and in each of us, that mental states become manifest in our everyday experience, that sickness originates in the mind, and that right thinking has a healing effect.

∞

The will may, indeed, work veritable wonders in a person—especially the highest form of will we call imagination. The will—and its manifestation as imagination—is capable of freeing those innate, healing energies that automatically work to regulate the health of every human organism, but which may easily become paralyzed by the slightest interference of negative thought. Thus, everything depends on how best to remove the shackles imposed by the influence of such thoughts.

Beyond all this, as is the case with all manifestations of the life force, we are dealing here with the tension between two opposing forces or polarities: On the one hand there is the inherent tendency of the cells to deteriorate and decline, which is a function of our physical, temporal nature; on the other there is the will to bring about healing, which arises out of the individual's spiritual nature.

In order for self-healing to occur, it is crucial that sick individuals externalize their will to recover; that is, detach themselves from it and experience it as something apart from themselves. In this way they can activate the tension between the will towards illness, which originates in the cells of the body, and the will to recover, which arises in the spiritual nature of the individual.

The stresses on the sick person are reduced to a minimum as soon as the spiritual will towards recovery—to bring order to that which is disordered in the organism—begins to have an effect. This is not always an easy thing to set in motion and at times it is almost impossible. At first, it may need to be stimulated into activity from an outside source.

This outside source may be a collective will, as it is present in places of pilgrimage, for example, or it may come from a single person. When a single individual is the source, its power depends upon the inherent ability of the individual to transmit this healing will to others.

❧

In the medical field it has often been noted that a particular method of healing can lead to the most satisfying results in the hands of one doctor whereas other doctors, no less diligent and using the same method, are hardly able to attain any results at all.

Indeed, breadth of knowledge and even an abundance of practical experience are no substitute for the inborn ability to heal. Individuals should only pursue the healing arts if they feel certain that they have the ability to transmit to others the spiritual will to recover from that which is diseased.

In contrast, if one has a purely scientific interest in the inner workings of the human organism and its different pathologies, one should pursue a career in research—which may then greatly benefit the patient in an indirect way. But where clinical medicine is concerned, one must differentiate between the aptitude for research and the aptitude for healing.

Both these aptitudes are innate: One must be *born* as a healer or as a researcher. Neither can be fully acquired through learning even though many doctors, born to be researchers, have found it necessary to treat patients. Often they are motivated by the humane desire to help those who have turned to them in need and thus, at times, many patients have indeed been healed.

It is extremely rare to find both these aptitudes in one person and so I will not comment
on this here.

∞

Of course, researchers must be able to study
illnesses directly in patients, but it should
surely be possible for them to leave the actual
healing to those who are born healers.

Today we have intricate methods with which to
assess whether a person is suited to be a loco-
motive driver or pursue some other technical
vocation. It should certainly also be possible
to ascertain whether a student of medicine
is more suited to becoming a researcher or a
clinician. If such methods were used in the
healing arts, we would surely find that there
are enough born healers among us to fill every
need.

If all medical doctors were indeed born healers, it would hardly happen that some obscure
"miracle worker" could acquire a reputation
for being able to cure all kinds of illnesses
which medically trained doctors cannot.

Born healers are able to cure with any method
they choose and they will always balance

their scientific knowledge with their intuitive insights.

But as long as people do not understand that the right doctor must, above all, be a born healer, all innovations and reforms in the art of healing will be of limited benefit. The world will always pay attention when some true healer appears but, as long as we have doctors who are not true healers, confidence in the healing arts grounded in science will be undermined.

When people react in this way it is because they can instinctively sense the power to heal in those born to such a calling. They care little whether such individuals also have scientific training or are guided by medical standards of care.

Sick people want to be healed and do not want to be regarded as "interesting cases" by researchers or uninspired doctors. No true healer would ever see them that way.

❧

CHAPTER TEN

THE DANGERS
OF MYSTICISM

Historical documents from every age tell us of certain individuals who claim that their faith in the divine is based not only on religious beliefs but, much more so, on a certainty born of inner experience—and that this experience can only come about through special preparation.

Those who place their firm—yet unsubstantiated—trust in the axiom that "all human beings are equal before God" generally consider this claim to be arrogant. This is because they interpret "equality" before God to mean that every experience is equally accessible to everyone, even without this special preparation.

Nevertheless, we know from the reports of those who have had spiritual experiences that the range of inner experiences among human beings can vary considerably, just as we know that the ability to experience things in the external world can vary from person to person.

In the external world, the attributes individuals are born with and the extent to which they are able to develop their inborn potential affects their experience of that world. With regard to the world of Spirit and the experiences of the soul, a whole set of other factors come into play as well. All these must harmonize and work together if trustworthy experiences are to be had in the invisible realm.

≪

Instances of human beings who have experienced aspects of the realm of Spirit with complete clarity and certainty are extremely rare, but it would be foolish to disregard them or deny that they have really happened—simply because they are rare. Indeed, there are individuals, even today, who experience the Spirit in full waking consciousness and who are able to evaluate what they have experienced.

One must always distinguish, however, between what such individuals have actually experienced and how they attempt to communicate this experience in words.

In these attempts at communication, people fervently try to express that which can never be expressed in words and must therefore find images and metaphors that will help other souls grasp what they have experienced.

Those who have had the ineffable experience know intuitively that it will in some way also be valuable and inspiring to others; hence the desire to find a way to impart its essence.

At the same time they know with certainty that this experience is inaccessible to most, yet feel a duty—even though it may be difficult—to bear witness to what they have experienced.

⋇

When one considers the images and metaphors used in such personal accounts, one might easily assume that the same inner experience is being described and that the only differences stem from the particular individual's ability to draw from the treasury of words and world of images available to him or her.

Upon closer examination, however, even those who have never had such experiences will have no difficulty seeing that these personal accounts describe quite *different* experiences, even if the words and imagery used could lead one to suppose that they are essentially the same.

Indeed, one will soon discover that vastly different types of experiences are being described even though the same or similar words are being used to depict them.

Since all experiences of the realm of Spirit are beyond the grasp of the physical senses, they can only be alluded to using images and metaphors—and this only with difficulty. Therefore, those who attempt to make them understandable will gratefully adopt the images and metaphors of others in their desire to express the inexpressible.

⁂

Experiences of the radiant realm of the Spirit can be divided into two groups, each connoting a different type of experience, and each of these groups encompasses a range of distinct, individual experiences.

In one group are those whose experience is subjective: They experience that which is hidden in their own innermost being, but believe this to be an experience of the divine.

This is because they do not know the vastness of the heights, depths, and breadth that the human soul encompasses and are unwilling to expand their vision and see that all this is still a part of being human.

Such experiences are usually ecstatic or visionary in nature, and always occur in an altered state that is very different from normal, waking consciousness.

In the second group are those who experience *objective* spiritual Reality and who instinctively shy away from all ecstasies and visions. They accept an experience as being valid only if they can attain it with unclouded physical senses, while remaining conscious of themselves and the world around them.

These individuals are far more rare than those who have visions or ecstatic experiences because fully conscious experiences of the Spirit require strict inner training and self-control. Such individuals must lead healthy, ordered inner lives and refrain from indulging in feelings of euphoria. They should approach their efforts with a sober attitude yet filled with reverence for the living Spirit. Only then can they be certain that their experience will be unadorned and pure and not embroidered with their own imaginative interpretations or fantasy.

One must carefully differentiate between these two main groups if one is to correctly evaluate the countless reports from ancient and modern times that testify to actual or supposed experiences of the divine.

It is not too difficult to make this distinction.

Ecstatics and visionaries always present their experiences in a way that confirms the religious beliefs of their time; at best, they seek to expand or deepen such beliefs. By contrast, the writings of those who give witness to the pure experience of spiritual Reality clearly show that they have liberated themselves from the shackles of earth-bound, conventional thinking.

They may often refer to the prevailing beliefs of the time, but only because using references that are familiar makes it easier for others to understand what they are conveying.

When they use terms and concepts generally accepted in their world, it is not their intention to support beliefs about spiritual matters that are prevalent in their time and place. Rather, based on the strength of insight they have gained and unconcerned about any edifice built of dogma, they show which building blocks of such an edifice are of enduring value and which are not—which have been correctly hewn and which have not. It is never their intention to tear down any edifice but, rather, to insure that it conforms to the Reality that they know through their own objective, spiritual experience.

⚭

Much confusion has resulted from the uncritical mixing of accounts from the two major groups I have just described.

While the testimonies of ecstatics and visionaries may at times be worthy of admiration and even high esteem, they are always subjective and conditioned by the time in which they were written. They are opaque and imprecise accounts of an uncommon personal experience which is by no means free of deception. They may be compared to the writings of a poet, but without the majesty that comes from an artist whose command of words and images brings beauty and coherent form to their creation.

The value of reading such testimonials lies in the inspiration one can feel from their poetry and the elation one can experience from identifying with the religious fervor of the writer—but nothing more.

When regarded with detachment, these testimonials, although significant and compelling, are filled with human error. Their real value lies solely in that they provide material for research, even if they strike us as deeply moving, grand, or simply foolish.

The mysticism that is rooted in religious beliefs and dogmas, which has been marveled at in every age and by all peoples, has spread like weeds in fertile soil. As a result, it is almost impossible to speak of genuine mystical experiences anymore because every flower of true mysticism has been crowded out by this invasive overgrowth.

If this devalued word is to regain its integrity so that it may once again aid in understanding, it will be necessary to clearly distinguish between experiences that merely appear to be mystical and those that truly are: to recognize those true, mystical experiences through which the human spirit knows itself within the timeless realm of radiant Spirit.

It is possible to do this even if one still feels some reverence for certain accounts of "mystical" experiences because of their literary value.

∽

Ultimately, readers of mystical accounts are motivated by the desire to penetrate to a deeper, clearer and, above all, truer understanding of the cosmology of the spiritual world that awaits us as eternal Reality. Therefore, identification with "mystical" testimonials that are influenced by religious systems and their dogmatic beliefs is almost always—if not always—a danger for those who do not know how to distinguish between true and pseudo-mysticism and are not strong enough to break with long-cherished ideas for the sake of truth. This truth can only be found in the reports of individuals who have gained entry into the radiant realm of Spirit while fully awake, clear-headed and calm.

It should be obvious in which of these two groups I include myself since, in my writings, I have always emphasized how far I am from entertaining ecstasies or visions. Nevertheless, if one wishes to categorize me as a mystic, for lack of a better word, then I must insist that one distinguish between mysticism that is tied to religious dogmas and mystical experience that is grounded in the spiritual Reality within the cosmos. I believe that I have now made the need for this distinction sufficiently clear.

To those who look to the writings of those "mystics" who are bound by religious dogma in order to find confirmation of the teachings I offer in my writings I say: spare yourselves the effort.

They may come across certain points of agreement in these two kinds of writings but they will far more likely be confused by quite a different, if not diametrically opposite, use of words and images.

Most importantly, they should realize that their need to find confirmation for my words in another source proves, in and of itself, that they are still far from having understood my teachings.

∞

A new day of spiritual awakening is dawning and no earthly power, no matter how firmly entrenched or time-honored, can hold it back. But in this generation, only those who hasten to greet the day with free and sober minds will behold it and only they can understand my teachings.

In writing these books, it is not my intention to attract followers and I am grateful to each of my readers who take as little notice as possible of their author.

It has become my task in this life to write down what I am destined to give to my fellow human beings, while remaining in obscurity. I have nothing to offer other than these insights into the human being's relationship to the realm of the living Spirit.

∞

POEMS

1. THE INNER TEMPLE

Stand with both feet on the earth—
do not float in the air unmoored.
But if you would seek the primordial
Ground of All Being
you must descend into the depths
where clouds pour forth their floods
onto earth's waiting lap;
where in glowing fires of love
Male and Female join in joyful purity;
where the procreative forces
ever fructify this earth.
Turn to where the towering ancients
once sought life's primordial stream.
Know that only blest are they
who have bathed in its waters
and have cleansed themselves
of life's daily dust.
Faith alone will let them enter here.

2. OUTER AND INNER

Just as the world of the physical senses
can become known only to those
who move within it
And so moving, find themselves
enclosed by it—
In this way too the world of the Spirit
can become known only to those
who have prepared the way for the Spirit
to unfold
inside themselves
expanding infinitely in order to enclose it
Thus they are not merely part of the world
they behold
but also hold it within their own Being
No border separates
the one who is experiencing
from that which is experienced
Beholder and beheld are one

3. WISDOM

Self-sustaining
perfect in itself
timeless power
lives within the soul
forming itself
into Life divine
Never was it born
never can it die
Those who recognize it
recognize *themselves*
and live their Life everlasting
within their own being
They do not fear
that they might perish

4. ALONE AND TOGETHER

One single Life
unites us in its glow
and this Life belongs to each of us
alone.
What we have to give each other
is always the same
and yet
it will always be different...

5. WATER

The ocean's wave has healing power—
river, rain and morning dew
nourish forest, field and meadow
From water all life flows.

Yet more is told of here
pouring forth
from Spirit's eternal source
No human tongue can speak of it
Only those who are awake can learn of it
Earth's miracle
unfathomable to all who seek to understand it
with the mind.

To know the power of water
is to know its holiness
Nowhere does the Spirit show its sacred
mysteries more
than when it flows down upon the earth
and from water creates new birth.

6. IT IS NOT EASY

It is not so easy to change your thinking
such that you can recognize your *self*
in what is meant when you say "I"
So that when descending in your being
into deep meditation
you will find the One who has no name.

It is not easy to recognize the One in Many
and to dwell in the Oneness
And without renouncing the self
to drive out the last impulse towards pretense
from its paradise.

7. THE ETERNAL

Because it is so near
you do not see it
Because you look for it in the distance
your vision is beguiled.

And so you search
in the vastness of the cosmos
where no one who has not connected deeply
    within
where no one who has not descended deeply
    into the self
has ever found it
Until the jewel offers itself to the soul.

8. SINFONIA

From fiery suns ablaze with primordial Light
pour seeds that sprout into suns
that turn into centers of cosmic solar systems
that grow into planets that orbit many suns.

On planets beings germinate
Sublime spirits who have fallen
join them in pre-destined union
Thus united
these spirits draw the earth-born upward
And now hosts of silent human spirits
rise steadily to the stars
turn into spiritual suns
to illuminate those still dwelling on the earth
from afar.

9. MYSTERIUM MAGNUM

Until now your body's vigor
has merely been the source of sensual pleasure
That this same body
forms the body for the Spirit
is known by just a few.

Nature, ever secretive,
hides her wonders
under many layers
And yet she leaves some hints
for those who will
fulfill her laws.

This is the Mystery
that leads Male and Female
to unite
in love's glowing passion
And create a new body for the Spirit
from timeless, radiant flames.

10. HOMECOMING

I too was once spellbound
by the world of appearances.
I too was once entranced
by the world of dreams.
But then within the Light
I was enkindled
and *became* light—
and rose upward in its radiance.

Now the darkness of the earth around me
appears to me a dim haze in the distance.
In the abyss I still hear the roaring
of a raging sea
and yet my star is undisturbed.

11. ANTAGONISM

Often when I speak
sacred, earnest words
about sublime things
A base creature creeps
across my path
and smirks.

Yet I am careful not to scold
if it feigns familiarity
Because in realms sublime
kindness is extended even to the lowly.

12. FOOLISH SEEKERS

What is the meaning of this or that
and how are they related?
Never-ending are their questions
But what to do and what eschew
this they never ask
Because they only seek to feed the mind
they fail to feed the soul
They learn the teachings just as children
learn their schoolroom lessons
but very far are they
from practicing what they have learned in life.

They think themselves to be initiates
and preen themselves in front of others
Self-hypnotized, they feel themselves
awash in bliss
Always ready to lecture and expound
their blather leaves the truth in tatters
Alas! How far they are from clarity
and everything that matters.

13. FALSE DIGNITY

My friend, your dignity does not become you
you have become its slave
In times past you walked with upright gait
you took chances and sometimes succeeded
But now you walk bent over
and everything you do seems false
Please ask yourself
if you still dare to be yourself
as you were in times gone by
My friend, you are becoming a misery
to yourself
and a misery to others
who would gladly have walked by your side
Your pathos rings false
you have made a mockery of all that is best
in you
My friend, turn away
from such pretentious striving
if you would lift yourself up to the Spirit
You must first master your ego
if ever you are to achieve something worthy
However great you think yourself to be

so long as you are mastered by your
self-importance
you will remain petty and small
In the end you will only be
what you appear to be
and never will you truly *be*
You will remain lying on the ground
and never learn to fly

14. INNER DISCIPLINE

Many things you must
cast out
from within
if you would keep your innermost pure
Only take in and remember
those things
that are pristine

15. TO MY WELL-INTENTIONED FRIENDS

There are people who would like me to be
different
not quite the way I really am
And truly, these good people
mean well
And if I really were to be the way
they want me to
I truly would not look so bad at all
But this is not who I was meant to be
and I do not wish to step out of my skin
Had I been made according to their plan for me
I would not be myself
And if I were to become their puppet
and shape myself according to their wishes
No good or gain would come to anyone

16. ALIGNMENT

If your arrow is intended for the eagle
you must aim high at the heavens
If your striving is for the sublime
look upwards to the worlds on high
and do not be deterred
when you encounter clouds

17. LETTING GO

Only when they can let the loved one go
only then will the wise give their love.

If a friend extends a hand
those who are wise will gladly take it
And if that friend wishes to leave
the wise will let go with a blessing.

Wise ones know from the start
that the gift of friendship
is always a loan
never one's possession.

18. BLOSSOM OR FRUIT

Those who would enjoy
blossoms in their vases
may not demand fruits
when the branch withers—
For all branches without roots will wither...

19. ONE THING AT A TIME

Always trying to do
everything at once
even if you can do it
means that you will always overshoot the mark.
One rides on a saddle horse
and ploughs with a plough horse.

20. KNOW-IT-ALLS

Some think they know better
than what others have tried to tell them
And so they sharpen their knives
and cut into fruits they have never seen before
They cut slices in all sizes
and leave the core with the seeds hanging from it
They take these slices home
and plant them in their gardens
In their dreams they see the slices sprout
But, alas, despite all their patient waiting
they water their gardens in vain

21. ARROGANT ONES

Just ignore their stupid chatter—
let them feel so very self-important
Let them draw their false conclusions
and bask in righteous indignation.

Have pity on these wretches
with their limited horizons
One must feel compassion for them
since they never seem to learn.

Whatever they themselves have not conceived of
does not exist for them
With shallow words they denigrate
what gives wings to others
Dearly will they pay
for their false conclusions
They will only ever see the shell
and never find the nut within.

22. ADVICE

Accept your life just as it is—
Do not feel it should be different
Do not curse a single day
Shoulder all that comes your way
Bless whatever this life brings you
And you will be blessed in turn

For a deeper understanding
of the core of Bô Yin Râ's teachings
you may want to read:

The Book on the Living God,
The Book on Life Beyond and
The Book on Human Nature

These three books should be
read together.

A description of all three books follows.

The Book on the Living God

The Book on the Living God describes the inner path that leads to birth of the Living God within—what we must do and what to avoid on the long journey towards awakening the consciousness of our timeless self.

Ordinary consciousness, Bô Yin Râ tells us, is actually like sleep; there is a greater consciousness that is alive in us, informing every cell, and our task is to unite it with our self-awareness.

We must also set aside the ideas we have been taught about an anthropomorphic God. God is not meant to be an external object of worship but, rather, an experience to be awakened within us. We are cautioned to avoid the pitfalls that might divert us: following false teachers or believing that certain foods or exercises, or ecstatic experiences, have spiritual merit. Everyday life, when lived with attention to the ultimate goal, will lead us towards a gradual awakening of our timeless self.

E.W.S. Publisher

Contents: Word of Guidance. "The Tabernacle of God is with Men." The White Lodge. Meta-Physical Experiences. The Inner Journey. The En-Sof. On Seeking God. On Leading an Active Life. On "Holy Men" and "Sinners." The Hidden Side of Nature. The Secret Temple. Karma. War and Peace. The Unity among Religions. The Will to Find Eternal Light. The Human Being's Higher Faculties of Knowing. On Death. On the Spirit's Radiant Substance. The Path toward Perfection. On Everlasting Life. The Spirit's Light Dwells in the East. Faith, Talismans, and Images of God. The Inner Force in Words. A Call from Himavat. Giving Thanks. Epilogue.

The Book on Life Beyond

The Book on Life Beyond is a guide to help readers understand what they can expect to find in the life beyond death, and how to best prepare for it.

Bô Yin Râ explains that life beyond is actually another dimension of the same life we know here on earth—just as real and solid, but perceived through spiritual, rather than our limited, physical senses. He emphasizes the direct connection between our actions here on earth and their effects on life beyond. We bring with us into life beyond the same state of inner being with which we departed, and are able to experience its wonders exactly to the degree to which we have developed our spiritual self. For example, those who have failed to show compassion for others and have lived selfishly will find that life beyond lacks the warmth and light that other, more developed souls can perceive.

Bô Yin Râ counsels us to mentally practice the "art of dying" as a meditative practice to prepare for the transition from physical to spiritual existence. The goal is to constantly orient one's thinking, emotions and desires toward transformation of the self, in order to be able to receive the spiritual help that will be available to us after death.

E.W.S. Publisher

Contents: Introduction. The Art of Dying. The Temple of Eternity and the World of Spirit. The Only Absolute Reality. What Should One Do?

The Book on Human Nature

The Book on Human Nature presents basic concepts about
human nature with the goal of inspiring readers to awaken
the timeless, spiritual spark within. We become fully human
only when the spiritual potential within us gradually awak-
ens and infuses our material, purely animal selves. It is a
path that every human being may and should pursue.

A central understanding is that all life results from the
joining of opposites, in particular, the polarity of male
and female energies. Bô Yin Râ emphasizes that the true
spiritual human being is male and female united in one
entity; when we seek our spiritual self, we must call forth
the male and female in ourselves and in all things. He dis-
cusses the biblical fall from grace as a descent from the
spiritual plane, in which male and female were united, onto
a material plane, in which male and female are split apart.

Bô Yin Râ warns men that holding onto the illusion of male
superiority means forfeiting their spiritual life. While the
spiritual paths that are natural for men and women are
different in tone—open and receptive for women, active
and grasping for men—they are equal and complementary.
He tells us that *true* marriage is preparation for the life
beyond: by coordinating the desires, wills and attitudes of
two beings we once again bring about, in some measure, the
original state in which male and female energies are united.

E.W.S. Publisher

Contents: Introduction. The Mystery Enshrouding Male
and Female. The Path of the Female. The Path of the
Male. Marriage. Children. The Human Being of the Age
to Come. Epilogue. A Final Word.

THE
KOBER
PRESS

* 9 7 8 0 9 1 5 0 3 4 3 2 1 *